THE PEANUT BUTTER

"I CAN'T GET ENOUGH OF IT"
COOKBOOK

HEALTHY, MOUTHWATERING RECIPES AND
FASCINATING FACTS FOR

PEANUT BUTTER LOVERS

JOYCE MACKIE

DISCLAIMER

Disclaimer and Terms of Use: Effort has been made to ensure that the information in this book is accurate and complete, however the author and the publisher do not warrant the accuracy of the information, text, or graphics contained within the book due to the rapidly changing nature of science, research, known and unknown facts, and the Internet.

Table of Contents

4

INTRODUCTION

Over the years, in my passion for peanut butter, I have sought many ways to include it in both new dishes and old favorites. I have gathered recipes, adapted them, and created my own, always choosing easier, more healthful options. I have omitted refined sugar, trans fat and, in most recipes, gluten, and substituted more nutritious and flavorful ingredients. Sometimes I converted recipes that required cooking into raw versions that retained beneficial enzymes and other essential nutrients without sacrificing taste. As a result, I soon had a collection of recipes that I felt compelled to share with those who love peanut butter as much as I do.

As you look through the recipes, don't be surprised if your mouth begins to water and you have an urge to go eat a spoonful of peanut butter. If you are one of those people who can't get enough peanut butter, you may want to start your day with a Peanut Butter and Jelly Smoothie, have Superfood Balls for a midmorning snack, eat the Beet Salad for lunch, end the day with Baked Squash, and enjoy Peanut Butter Chocolate Mousse for dessert, all gluten-, sugar- and dairy-free.

Peanut butter isn't just about breakfast and snacks and yummy desserts; it also has a story to tell—of centuries of becoming more than just a squashed peanut, of feeding the poor and undernourished, and years later, of becoming a favorite food of some of the well-to-do. In the first part of this book, you'll enjoy reading these stories about peanut butter and discovering just how popular it has become. In the second part, you'll find the recipes.

Have you been searching for healthy snacks for your kids? They'll love the Frozen Peanut Butter and Banana Pops and the Bite-sized Brownies. (When you make them, be sure to leave some for the kids.) They'll be thrilled to discover the Nori Roll-ups or Chocolate Peanut Butter Leather in their lunch boxes.

If sugar is your concern, look no further. Every recipe, except one, is free of processed sugar. You'll be delighted with the Chocolate Peanut Butter Pie and Peanut Butter Chocolate Cheesecake. And for those times when you do want to indulge your sweet tooth with something sweet and gooey, the Butter Tarts, made with coconut sugar and maple syrup, are just the thing.

While you're enjoying these delectable recipes, you will feel good knowing that, in your quest for more peanut butter, you've made wise choices that your body will thank you for.

PART ONE—ABOUT PEANUT BUTTER

THE STORY OF PEANUT BUTTER

You may think that peanut butter is a fairly recent U.S. invention, but there is evidence that early forms of a similar food made from peanuts were eaten centuries ago. For many years before peanuts found their way to other countries, South Americans had been grinding them into a paste to supplement their diet. Archaeologists found peanuts at a 3800-year-old site in Peru. Eventually, the Spaniards and Portuguese transported peanuts to Africa and then, in the 16th century, to India.

Not until the 17th century were peanuts introduced to Eastern America via slave ships from Africa. By the 18th century, peanuts were found everywhere in the world that they could be grown.

In the early-to-mid 19th century in the U.S., shelled roasted peanuts were chopped, ground, beaten in a cloth bag, and eaten with salt. In 1884, Canadian Marcellus Gilmore Edson was the first to patent a peanut paste made from roasted peanuts.

Around 1894 in the U.S., a physician George A. Bayle was instrumental in marketing a peanut paste as a protein supplement for those who couldn't chew meat. Later, John Harvey Kellogg made peanut butter from steamed peanuts for patients in his sanitarium and, in 1897, patented a process for making peanut butter from boiled peanuts.

In the 1890s, peanut butter-making machines were developed by Joseph Lambert and Ambrose Straub.

Interestingly, the boll weevil played a significant role in the story of peanut butter. In the early 20th century, the insect destroyed many cotton crops, forcing farmers to turn to peanuts as an alternative cash crop. When the volume of peanuts on the market was dramatically increased as a consequence, production of peanut butter also increased.

In 1904, peanut butter was brought to the attention of many Americans when C. H. Summer sold it from a booth at the World's Fair in St. Louis, where it met with phenomenal success. In the same year, Beech Nut became the first company to sell peanut butter nationally, and five years later, Heinz became the second. By 1914, several dozen brands had appeared on the market.

Between 1921 and 1923, methods for hydrogenating peanut butter were developed to prevent the separation of the oil and solids in peanut butter, allowing peanut butter to safely be stored longer. This extended shelf life was a boon to many people without refrigeration, and thus the popularity of peanut butter grew.

In the following years, new products containing peanut butter began to appear on the market. Crunchy peanut butter was first introduced circa 1933-35, and today, coarse and grainy textures are also available.

In 1928, H. B. Reese created the now-famous Reese's peanut butter cups in the basement of his home. Later, his company, H. B. Reese Candy Co., merged with Hershey Chocolate Corporation. Reese's peanut butter sticks, peanut butter eggs, hearts, pumpkins, baking chips, and toppings are now sold. Peanut butter cups are available in milk, white, or dark chocolate, regular or sugar-free, and in sizes ranging from mini to a huge eight ounces.

During World War II, peanut butter was included in GI rations. The GIs acquired a taste for it and later introduced the product to their families, thereby increasing the demand for peanut butter. After the war,

13

new harvesting equipment revolutionized the peanut industry and contributed to the boom in peanut butter sales.

As more varied products billed as peanut butter entered the market, the U.S. Food and Drug Administration felt it necessary to establish a standard whereby peanut butter had to contain at least 90% peanuts and could not contain artificial flavors, colors, or chemical preservatives. Peanut products containing less than the minimum 90% would have to be called spreads.

In the early 21st century, many new products featuring peanut butter were introduced: ready-to-eat snacks, health bars, and candy. Peanut butter became available in many forms, including honey-roasted, low-fat, low-salt, low-sugar, added omega 3 oil, added jelly, and dehydrated.

The history of peanut butter has not been without challenges. In the early 1970s, the first salmonella contamination of peanut butter took place in Chicago, and outbreaks in other areas occurred in 2006-2009 and 2012. Unsanitary conditions in some of the old factories, which had not been upgraded for many years, appear to have been the main cause.

Nineteen ninety-six brought additional health concerns about peanut butter—allergies, aflatoxin, choking. The Peanut Institute was created in the U.S. to sponsor research and promote the healthy aspects of peanuts and peanut butter. Through the efforts of the Institute, unfavorable public opinion and declining sales were successfully reversed.

Another temporary setback for peanut butter sales was caused by severe drought conditions across the Southern U.S. in 2010 and again in 2011. The drought decimated the peanut crop in that area, resulting in a peanut shortage and, in many areas, soaring peanut butter prices.

In spite of the challenges through the years, peanut butter has survived and continues to be a staple in many households: indeed, some of us wouldn't ever want to be without it.

DID YOU KNOW?

Arachibutyrophobia is the fear of peanut butter sticking to the roof of one's mouth.

The Latin name for peanuts means "weed whose fruit grows underground."
Names for peanuts include goobers, monkey nuts, groundpeas, and grunea seeds. The name "goober" comes from an African word. In India, peanuts were originally called "Mozambique beans."

Peanuts are actually a vegetable (legume) grown from a low bush about eighteen inches high or from a spreading vine. When the petals fall from the plants' yellow flowers, the buds, called "pegs," that are left behind find their way into the soil and develop into peanuts underground.

Harvesting peanuts can be challenging. The plants have to be dug up at a particular stage in their maturity, turned over, and left to dry before collecting. The weather is crucial in this drying process.

Once harvested, the peanuts are sent to factories, where they are cleaned and carefully inspected for aflatoxin, a naturally occurring carcinogenic toxin produced by a mold on the peanut shell.

After the peanuts are roasted and cooled, vegetable oil, salt, sugar, or dextrose may be added. Some manufacturers remove the peanut heart and skin, which can give a bitter taste to peanut butter. The difference in taste of peanut butter brands is due not only to what is removed from or added to the peanut butter, but also to the variety of peanut used.

Peanut butter is made from many types of peanuts. Some companies use more than one type of peanut in their butter. Runners and Virginias originate from one branch of the peanut family, while Spanish and Valencias are from another. Virginias, the peanuts sold in ballparks, is the largest type of peanut but is seldom used in peanut butter now.

Valencias are the only ones to have three or more peanuts in a shell. They are the sweetest and require more care and attention to farm than other types of peanuts. Deaf Smith peanut butter was the first to use Valencias (around 1970) and the first to market organic peanut butter. In the years that followed, Trader Joe's,

Sunland, MaraNatha, Once Again, and the Costco brand, Kirkland, began using Vlencias and many still do.

Spanish peanuts, used by Santa Cruz and Krema, are high in oil content and believed by some to have the best flavor. They make up only about 4% of the U.S. crop.

Many peanut butter companies use Runners because of their higher yield and higher number of peanuts per shell. Today, 99% of the peanuts grown in Georgia, the biggest U.S. peanut-growing state, are Runners.

PEANUT BUTTER AROUND THE WORLD TODAY

Peanut butter is popular in the U.S., Canada, Holland, Germany, and Saudi Arabia.

According to some sources, peanut butter is gaining popularity in Eastern Europe and is sometimes homemade there in places where it cannot be purchased.

Peanut butter in Haiti is called "mamba", and one variety is flavored with hot peppers.

In the Netherlands, peanut butter is called peanut cheese (pindakas) because the dairy farmers there don't want anything except butter made from milk to be called "butter."

The world's oldest brand of peanut butter, Sanitarium, has been made in Austria since 1898.

Kraft peanut butter is sold in Canada and Australia, but not in the U.S.

Some stores, in locations such as Boston, New York City, and Woburn, Mass., sell primarily peanut butter and related products.

Ready-to-use therapeutic foods (RUTFs) made with a form of peanut butter have been developed to feed the world's hungry. They are a low-cost, nutritious food containing peanut paste and milk powder, enriched with vitamins and minerals. One of the most popular is called Plumpy'nut.

Space Food Sticks, a type of energy food made of peanut butter, were developed as a food for astronauts. Astronaut Peggy Whitson said that during the year she spent aboard the international space station, her favorite food was peanut butter.

U.S. and Canadian customs do not allow airline passengers to carry more than 3.4 ounces of peanut butter in carry-on baggage. On one flight from Canada, I had to give up my precious jar of peanut butter at U.S. customs. (I had the option of going back through security and checking it in.)

Elvis Presley popularized peanut butter with his famous grilled bacon, peanut butter, and banana sandwiches. He was also known to fly to Denver with his friends for giant "Fool's Gold Loaf" sandwiches made from whole loaves of bread hollowed-out and spread generously with peanut butter and blueberry jelly, then filled with a pound of crisp bacon.

Ernest Hemingway is said to have liked peanut butter sandwiches containing thick onion slices.

Other famous people reported to love peanut butter include: Cher, Michael J. Fox, Madonna, Julia Roberts, Bill Clinton, Gerald Ford, Bill Cosby, Dan Rather, and Barbara Walters

In the 1982 movie "E.T. the Extra-Terrestrial," Elliott uses Reese's Pieces to lure E.T. The great success of this movie led to hugely increased sales for Reese's products. It is reported that Mars Candy Co. had earlier turned down an offer to use M & M's in the movie.

A German zoo once tried to lure a runaway kangaroo back into captivity by spreading his favorite food, peanut butter, on nearby trees and bushes.

The year after a record peanut crop in 1991, The National Peanut Council of America presented Russia with its first peanut butter and jelly sandwiches. (Some children thought the peanut butter was rather salty.) The Peanut Council, interested in helping to relieve food shortages in Russia, and to find a market for its own peanut surplus, donated thirty tons of peanuts to the country.

When the 1999 Tour de France USPS cycling team was unable to find any peanut butter in France, Jif sent them a supply of Jif Smooth Sensations, blends of peanut butter with chocolate, berries, and cinnamon apple.

In 2013, peanut butter was used in a diagnostic test to detect Alzheimer disease by measuring the subjects' ability to smell peanut butter through each nostril. The results of this study were reported in 2013 by researchers from the University of Florida's McKnight Brain Institute and published in the Journal of the Neurological Sciences.

Peanut and peanut butter festivals have been held in Alabama, Texas, and Virginia. At one, a prize was offered to the person who could make a sculpture entirely from peanut butter.

Peanut butter celebrations in the U.S. in 2015 included: Peanut Butter Fudge Day, Peanut Butter and Jelly Day, and Peanut Butter Cookie Day.

PEANUT BUTTER STATISTICS

Seventy-five percent of all peanuts are produced by (in order) India, China, Nigeria, the U.S., and Senegal. In China and India, they are used primarily for peanut oil.

Canada, Mexico, and Europe account for over 80% of U.S. peanut exports.

Canada is by far the largest importer of peanut butter. Ninety-four percent of Canadians have peanuts or peanut butter in their homes. They eat a little more per capita than Americans.

The world's largest peanut butter factory produces 250,000 jars every day.

It takes approximately 540 peanuts to make a twelve-ounce jar of peanut butter.

Americans now spend almost $800 million a year on peanut butter.

Amount of peanut butter produced in the United States:

1911	22,000,000 pounds
1919	up to 176,000,000 pounds

2007-2008   1,000,000,000 pounds

Americans eat more than 700 million pounds of peanut butter per year, about 3.3 pounds per person. (I eat approximately 15 pounds per year.)

Americans consume enough peanut butter annually to make more than ten billion peanut butter and jelly sandwiches. In 2010, Grand Saline, Texas won the title for the world's largest peanut butter and jelly sandwich (1342 pounds), breaking the record set in 1993 by Peanut, Pennsylvania's forty—foot-long sandwich, which contained a hundred and fifty pounds of peanut butter and fifty pounds of jelly. Since then, the record title has often been claimed, but not always officially.

The average American child will eat 1500 peanut butter sandwiches by the time they graduate from high school.

Six out of ten people prefer chunky peanut butter. Men seem to prefer chunky and women creamy. Grown-ups eat more peanut butter than kids.

In a September 2014 survey in which the Huffington Post asked what made the best peanut butter and jelly sandwich, the results were:

36% strawberry jelly

31% grape jelly

54% white bread

56% smooth peanut butter

80% liked crust left on the bread

PEANUT BUTTER NUTRITION FACTS

In addition to being low-cost and easy to use, peanut butter is healthy.

"Peanut butter is one of most nutritionally valuable foods available to the American public today." (The Peanut Butter Cookbook, William I. Kaufman)

Peanut butter with fruits or vegetables and milk is a balanced meal.

Peanuts are a legume, closely related to peas, beans, clover, and alfalfa.

The U.S. National Peanut Board reports that peanut butter contains more than thirty essential vitamins and minerals. It has a low glycemic index and is gluten-free. With 585 calories per 100 grams, it contains more protein, niacin, folate, and phytosterols per gram than any other nut. The antioxidant level in peanuts rivals that in blackberries and strawberries.

Roasted, salted peanuts are about 50% fat. A two-tablespoon serving

(28 grams) of peanut butter contains 12 grams of unsaturated fat, 2 grams of saturated fat, and no trans-fat. The main fatty acids are oleic and linoleic.

Originally, only hydrogenated oil was used in peanut butter, but now some brands use cheaper oils, which are often genetically modified. Be aware that even peanut butter labeled "natural" may contain palm oil (considered to be detrimental to your health and to the environment), sugar, evaporated cane juice, and salt. If a jar of peanut butter (even organic) contains less than .5 grams of trans fat *per serving,* the label can legally state that no trans fat is present.

Peanuts are 26% protein. Protein is essential for muscle growth and maintenance. Two tablespoons of peanut butter contains as much protein as one egg, a glass of milk, or a slice of cheese.

Peanut butter is a good source of Vitamin E (an antioxidant), phosphorus (important for cell growth), folate (needed for cell division), magnesium (vital for muscle function), copper (promotes red blood cell formation and healthy bones, nerves, and immune system), and fiber (which aids in digestion). It is an excellent source of niacin (a B vitamin that aids the digestive and nervous systems) and manganese (which helps process cholesterol and nutrients like carbohydrates and protein).

Other nutrients in peanut butter include potassium, resveratrol, iron, selenium, calcium, and zinc.

PART TWO—RECIPES

ABOUT THE INGREDIENTS

In some of these recipes, peanut butter is the star, while in others, it plays a supporting, but significant, role.

All of the recipes are vegetarian and most are vegan and gluten-free. The recipes abound with healthy superfoods. I use raw, unprocessed ingredients whenever possible. The exception is peanut butter. (I made raw peanut butter once and found it very hard to digest.)

All recipes are made with unsweetened organic peanut butter—Santa Cruz, Whole Foods' 365 brand, or Kirkland (Costco's brand). I add half a teaspoon of salt to an unsalted sixteen-ounce jar. I prefer crunchy style; if only smooth is available in the brand I want, I add chopped organic peanuts. (Before opening natural or organic peanut butter, turn the jar upside down for a day or two. The oil will rise in the jar and make it easier to stir.)

The outcome of any recipe depends, to a large degree, upon the quality of its ingredients. For optimum results, use the freshest and best you can afford.
A recipe may be different each time it is made—for example, the nuts may be drier, requiring more liquid than called for in the recipe. Each fruit and vegetable

differs from time to time in its flavor, and brands of peanut butter vary in taste and consistency.

You may find unfamiliar ingredients in some of the recipes, but a suitable substitution can often be made. Keep in mind that using a different ingredient may change the flavor or texture of the dish. If some ingredients are not available in your grocery store, they can usually be found in health food stores, Whole Foods, or at online retailers such as Amazon.

Many recipes are made using a food processor. In some cases, a high-speed blender or a hand mixer may be used instead, or the ingredients may be mixed by hand.

BUCKWHEAT FLOUR - This is a gluten-free flour. Gluten flours may be substituted in equal amounts.

CACAO POWDER - I recommend this for its intense, rich chocolate flavor and its antioxidants. The cocoa powder found in your local store may differ in flavor and bitterness, and using it may alter the recipe results.

CASHEW FLOUR - Grind cashews in a coffee grinder or high-speed blender. Using other nuts may change the flavor or texture and add oil to the dish.

COCONUT BUTTER - Adds to the flavor and texture of a recipe, but can be omitted. Look in health food stores for this.

COCONUT OIL - When substituting another oil, keep in mind that coconut oil may be used in a recipe for its flavor and/or because it will harden when refrigerated.

COCONUT SUGAR - This is an unrefined brown sugar with a caramel flavor made from dried coconut palm nectar. Regular brown sugar may be substituted.

GLUTEN-FREE OATMEAL - Found in health food stores and online. Regular oatmeal can be used.

GOJI BERRIES - This Asian superfood is high in protein, vitamin A, and
Vitamin C. It adds a pleasant, subtle flavor and a sweetness to foods. Look for it in health food stores and online.

HEMP SEEDS - Hemp is high in protein, magnesium, phosphorus, zinc, and iron, and is a good source of healthy fats. It has a nutty flavor similar to pine nuts. Ground sunflower seeds may be substituted.

MACA - This energizing, nutrient-dense whole food adds a malt-like flavor to foods. It is available in health food stores or online. In some recipes, it can be omitted, but to do so will alter the flavor and nutritional value of the dish.

MAPLE SYRUP - Not to be confused with pancake syrup, maple syrup is used for its flavor and pairs well with other foods, especially peanut butter and chocolate. Agave syrup is the best substitute.

SWEETENERS - The recipes in this book that are "sugar-free" do not contain refined white sugar, brown sugar, or cane sugar. Dried fruit, bananas, agave syrup, pure maple syrup, honey, or coconut sugar are used as sweeteners.

HOW TO MAKE YOUR OWN PEANUT BUTTER

This is silky-smooth and full of fresh flavor. If you want a grainy texture, blend for a shorter time. I used a Vita-Mix blender; a food processor will also work, but it will take longer. Experiment with various types of peanuts and with different oils, such as hemp, peanut, or coconut. Raw peanuts can be used, but like me, you may find them rather unpalatable.

Makes about 10 ounces.

2 cups roasted peanuts

1/4 teaspoon salt (optional)

1-2 tablespoons oil

Chopped peanuts (optional)

1. Place peanuts in a blender and process for about 30 seconds. Stop blender and, using a spatula, push peanuts from sides back onto blades. Repeat this process until you have a soft, but very grainy, butter.
2. Add 1 tablespoon oil and blend again. If you like grainy peanut butter, you may want to stop here. For a very smooth butter, you may need to add another half-tablespoon of oil and blend again.
3. To keep the oil from separating, store in the refrigerator.
4. For crunchy peanut butter, add chopped peanuts to the finished peanut butter and blend quickly to mix, or stir in by hand.

SHAKES AND SMOOTHIES

PEANUT BUTTER GREEN SMOOTHIE

Your body will love this.

GLUTEN- AND DAIRY-FREE, ALSO SUGAR-FREE IF THE CRANBERRIES ARE SWEETENED WITH APPLE JUICE.

Makes about 2 cups.

1 pear
1/2 cup coconut milk
1/2 cup water
1 tablespoon dried cranberries
1 tablespoon hemp seeds
1 heaping tablespoon peanut butter, salted
1 thin slice unpeeled lemon
2 cups Swiss chard, beet greens, or romaine lettuce, packed

Blend all ingredients in blender until smooth. Chill before serving.

PEANUT BUTTER AND JELLY SMOOTHIE

Tastes like peanut butter and jelly.

GLUTEN-FREE, DAIRY-FREE, SWEETENED WITH HONEY

Makes 1 serving.

2/3 cup fresh or frozen cranberries

1/4 cup grapefruit or orange pieces

1/2 cup banana, very ripe (but not overripe)

2 tablespoons raisins

2 tablespoons peanut butter

1/3 cup water

2-3 teaspoons honey

Blend all ingredients until smooth. Chill before serving.

PEANUT BUTTER BANANA SHAKE

Thick, creamy, and delicious

GLUTEN-FREE, DAIRY-FREE, SUGAR-FREE

Makes 1- 2 servings.

2 large bananas

1 cup coconut milk

1/3 cup peanut butter

3 dates

1/2 teaspoon vanilla

Blend all ingredients until smooth. Chill before serving.

PEANUT BUTTER CHOCOLATE SHAKE

Enjoy this any time of day.

GLUTEN-FREE, DAIRY-FREE, SUGAR-FREE

Makes 1 serving.

1 medium banana (5-6 inch)

1 1/2 tablespoons cacao

3 dates

2 tablespoons smooth, salted peanut butter

1/2 cup coconut or other nut milk

1/2 teaspoon vanilla

Add more milk if you like a thinner shake.

Blend all ingredients in blender and chill well before serving.

BREAKFASTS

CHAI GRANOLA

Enjoy the heart-warming flavor and aroma of chai paired with the nutty taste of peanut butter in this granola.

GLUTEN-FREE, DAIRY-FREE, SUGAR-FREE

Makes approximately 4 cups.

1/3 cup smooth peanut butter

1/3 cup raw honey

1/2 teaspoon vanilla

1/4 teaspoon cinnamon

1/4 teaspoon powdered ginger

1/4 teaspoon allspice

1/4 teaspoon cardamom

2 tablespoons dried coconut

1/8 teaspoon salt

2 cups gluten-free oatmeal

1/2 cup pecans, roughly chopped

3/4 cup dried fruit (any of: raisins, chopped figs, apricots, dates)

1. Heat peanut butter and honey in a saucepan until creamy. Remove from heat and mix in vanilla and spices.
2. Combine mixture with oats. Add dried fruit, coconut, and nuts and mix well with a large spoon or with your hands.
3. Spread out on Teflon-lined dehydrator sheet. Dehydrate at 105 degrees for 7-8 hours or dry in a shallow pan in oven at lowest temperature.
4. Cool, cover, and store at room temperature, or in the refrigerator to retain freshness.

QUINOA PORRIDGE WITH PEANUT BUTTER

When you want a change from your morning oatmeal, quinoa is a very tasty alternative. To preserve its nutty taste and avoid a mushy texture, be careful not to overcook.

GLUTEN-FREE, DAIRY-FREE, SUGAR-FREE

Serves 2

1/2 cup quinoa, rinsed

1 cup water

2-3 tablespoons peanut butter

1 tablespoon hemp seeds

2 tablespoons raisins

1/4 teaspoon cinnamon

1/3 cup berries, sliced bananas, or other fruit

1/8 teaspoon salt (omit if peanut butter is salted)

1. Bring water to a boil. Stir in quinoa and salt, cover, and simmer on low approximately 20 minutes until quinoa is tender, removing it from heat before "tails" appear.
2. Remove from heat and stir in raisins, peanut butter, and cinnamon. Top with fruit and serve.

PEANUT BUTTER PRUNE PANCAKES

The toasted pecans add a lovely crunch to these hearty pancakes. To make oat flour, grind gluten-free oatmeal in a blender until fine. You can use any flour, but if you want to keep these gluten-free, substitute buckwheat flour.

GLUTEN-FREE, DAIRY-FREE, SWEETENED WITH COCONUT SUGAR

Makes 2 large or 3 small pancakes

1/2 beaten egg

1/4 cup plus 1 tablespoon coconut or other nut milk

1/4 teaspoon cinnamon (optional)

1 tablespoon creamy peanut butter

1/4 teaspoon coconut sugar

1/4 cup gluten-free oat flour

1 tablespoon coconut flour

1/8 teaspoon salt (1/4 teaspoon if peanut butter is unsalted)

3/4 teaspoon baking powder

1/16 teaspoon baking soda

2 large prunes or figs, chopped

1-2 tablespoons chopped pecans

1/2 tablespoon coconut oil for frying

Butter and syrup for serving

1. Whisk together egg, milk, cinnamon, peanut butter, and sugar.
2. In a separate bowl, mix flours, salt, baking powder, and soda.
3. Gently stir dry ingredients and prunes into the wet mixture. Do not over-mix. Batter will be thick.
4. Spoon gently into a hot frying pan to which coconut oil has been added. For a crispy edge on the pancakes, use more oil. Makes 2 or 3 cakes.
5. Fry over medium heat until bubbles form and cakes are brown on the underside, about 5 minutes.
6. Sprinkle chopped nuts on pancakes and turn them. The nuts will toast.
7. Turn heat down to low and cook for 2-3 minutes more. Be sure pancakes are cooked through.
8. Serve with butter and agave syrup or pure maple syrup.

APPLE BREAKFAST CAKE

Serve this with Peanut Butter Maple Syrup (recipe below) or pure maple syrup for a hearty, satisfying breakfast.

GLUTEN-FREE, DAIRY-FREE, SUGAR-FREE

Serves 2.

1 medium apple (peeled or unpeeled), grated

1/2 cup cooked millet

1/2 cup buckwheat flour

1/2 teaspoon baking soda

1/2 teaspoon salt

1/4 teaspoon cinnamon

2 tablespoons peanut butter

1 lightly beaten egg

1/4 -1/2 cup water, approximately

2 tablespoons coconut oil (for frying)

1. Mix together apple, millet, buckwheat flour, soda, salt, cinnamon, and peanut butter.
2. To the mixture, add the egg and enough water to make a batter like a thick porridge.

3. Spoon batter into a hot, oiled 10-12-inch frying pan. Cook until almost done. To turn cake, place a plate over the pan, turn pan upside down to transfer cake to the plate, and then slide pancake back into pan. Lower heat and finish cooking.

4. Serve with Maple Peanut Butter Syrup.

Peanut Butter Maple Syrup

2 tablespoons peanut butter

4 tablespoons pure maple syrup

2 tablespoons water

1/8 teaspoon vanilla (optional)

Whisk all ingredients together. If desired, heat before serving.

SNACKS

FROZEN BANANA POPS

The refreshing taste of an ice-cream bar and loaded with nutrition. Adapted from a recipe by Sharon Kobayashi in "A Sweet Dash Of Aloha."

GLUTEN-FREE, DAIRY-FREE, SUGAR-FREE

Makes about 12.

2 medium bananas
5 tablespoons water
3 pitted dates
1 1/2 tablespoons unsweetened peanut butter
1/8 cup cashew flour
1 teaspoon cacao
Squirt of lemon juice

1. Cut bananas into 2-inch pieces. Place a toothpick in the center of each piece. Arrange in a single layer on a baking pan lined with parchment paper and freeze solid.
2. Blend remaining ingredients in blender until smooth. Dip each frozen banana piece into the

coating and carefully return to the pan. Freeze solid.

3. For a thicker coating, dip once more and return to the freezer.

SUPERFOOD PEANUT BUTTER BALLS

A perfect combination of nutrition and taste. These are a favorite of mine. Use raw ingredients for the greatest nutritional benefit.

NO-COOK, SUGAR-FREE, GLUTEN-FREE, MOSTLY RAW INGREDIENTS

Makes about 18 balls if you don't eat too much of the mix while you're preparing them.

1/2 cup peanut butter

4 tablespoons raw hemp seeds

2 tablespoons raw sunflower seeds

4 tablespoons raw ground almonds

1 tablespoon raw ground pecans

1 tablespoon shredded coconut

1 tablespoon raw goji berries, ground into powder

1 teaspoon raw maca powder

1 tablespoon raw honey

4 chopped dried apricots

4 dried dates

1/2 teaspoon vanilla extract

Pinch of salt

Ground pecans for coating

1. Pulse all ingredients in food processor until the mixture holds together, or mix by hand.
2. Form into small balls. Coat with ground pecans. Refrigerate.

NORI PEANUT BUTTER ROLLUPS

Healthy, quick, and easy

GLUTEN-FREE, DAIRY-FREE, SWEETENED WITH HONEY

Makes 8.

2 sheets Nori

4 tablespoons peanut butter

4 teaspoons honey (optional)

1. With a sharp knife, cut Nori sheets into 2-inch wide strips.
2. Spread 1/2 teaspoon honey on each strip. Add about 1/2 tablespoon peanut butter to each strip.
3. Roll up strips and press to seal. Refrigerate.

Variation:

Place lengthwise slices of banana on peanut butter and honey before rolling up each strip.

PEANUT BUTTER BANANA CHOCOLATE LEATHER

A healthy treat that kids of all ages love.

GLUTEN-FREE, DAIRY-FREE, SUGAR-FREE

1 cup peanut butter

3 cups ripe bananas

2 tablespoons raw cacao powder

2 tablespoons raw coconut butter (optional)

1 teaspoon vanilla

1/2 cup chopped walnuts

1. Blend peanut butter, bananas, cacao, coconut butter, and vanilla in blender until smooth. Stir in walnuts.
2. Spread onto parchment paper or Teflon sheet of dehydrator tray. Dry   24-48 hours. Drying time will depend upon humidity, and the size and type of dryer. Leather should be dry to the touch when done.
3. If you don't have a dehydrator, these are worth trying out in your oven. Set the oven at its lowest temperature and leave the door ajar. However, be aware that your results may differ somewhat;

unlike your dehydrator, there is a lack of air flow in an oven.

4. Cut into 2-inch strips with a sharp knife and roll up. Refrigerate.

PEANUT BUTTER BANANA ORANGE LEATHER

Just as good as the chocolate leather.

GLUTEN-FREE, DAIRY-FREE, SUGAR-FREE

1 cup peanut butter

3 cups ripe bananas

Grated rind of one medium orange

1 teaspoon cinnamon

1. Blend all ingredients in blender until smooth.
2. Dry as in previous recipe.

APRICOT HUMMUS BALLS

A sweet and savory appetizer adapted from a recipe in "Alive" magazine.

GLUTEN- AND SUGAR-FREE

Serves 5-6

1 1/4 cup cooked chickpeas, drained and rinsed

1/4 cup chopped dried apricots

1 1/2 tablespoons peanut butter

1 tablespoon olive oil

2 tablespoons lemon juice

1/2 tablespoon chopped fresh rosemary

1/2 garlic clove, minced

1/4 teaspoon salt (less if peanut butter is salted)

1. Process chickpeas in food processor or blender until crumbly. Add remaining ingredients and continue to process until mixture holds together.
2. Form into 1-inch balls and place on baking sheet lined with parchment paper. Bake at 350 degrees for 12 minutes.
3. Serve with plain yogurt for dipping. Or, for a different dip, whisk together 3/4 cup plain

yogurt, 1/4 cup peanut butter, and 2 tablespoons agave or maple syrup.

SIX QUICK PEANUT BUTTER SNACKS:

1. Dates stuffed with peanut butter.
2. Peanut butter on a slice of cheese.
3. Peanut butter with cheese and dates.
4. Peanut butter with cheese and dates, rolled up in a lettuce leaf.
5. Peanut butter mixed with coconut butter, honey, and cacao powder.
6. Spread two slices of banana (sliced lengthwise) with peanut butter to make a sandwich. The banana is the "bread."

LUNCHES AND DINNERS

PEANUT BUTTER WRAPS

Spread 1/2 - 1 tablespoon peanut butter on a flour tortilla or lettuce leaf; top with an uncut banana. Roll up.

SEVEN PEANUT BUTTER SANDWICH IDEAS:

1. Peanut butter with raisins.
2. Peanut butter with raisins and chocolate chips.
3. Peanut butter with marshmallows.
4. Peanut butter and honey.
5. Peanut butter and banana on cinnamon raisin bread.
6. Peanut butter and mayonnaise (Southern Housekeeper, early 1900s).
7. Siamese sandwich - peanut butter, mayo, shrimp, raisins, apple, celery, onion, powdered ginger, and lime or lemon rind (Ladies Home Journal, 1968).

PEANUT BUTTER SAUCE

This sauce can be served over cooked noodles and pasta or gluten-free alternatives such as rice, millet, or quinoa. Add vegetables for a complete meal.

GLUTEN-FREE, DAIRY-FREE, SUGAR-FREE

Makes 1 cup.

3 1/2 tablespoons smooth peanut butter

1 1/2 tablespoons Bragg Liquid Aminos or soy sauce

2 cloves garlic, minced or chopped

1/2 cup coconut milk

1 tablespoon coconut sugar

1 tablespoon lemon juice

1/16 teaspoon cayenne

1/2 teaspoon finely chopped fresh ginger

Salt to taste

Blend all ingredients in blender until sauce is warm enough to serve, or mix ingredients and gently heat in a saucepan on stove until peanut butter is melted.

PEANUT BUTTER LETTUCE PARCELS

I like to put lots of peanut butter and a generous amount of filling in these.

GLUTEN-FREE

Makes 4-6

4-6 large leaves romaine lettuce or collard leaves

1/2 apple diced

1/4 cup diced celery

2 tablespoons raisins

2 tablespoons finely-diced Gouda cheese

2 tablespoons mayonnaise

1/2 teaspoon tahini

1/2 teaspoon Dijon mustard

Salt and pepper to taste

Peanut butter (about 1/2 tablespoon per wrap)

1. Mix all ingredients except lettuce and peanut butter.
2. Cut romaine or collard leaves in half lengthwise, removing rib.

3. Spread desired amount of peanut butter on one of the halves. Place other half on top, forming a cross.
4. Spoon a portion of the apple mixture onto the middle of the top leaf. Fold in the two peanut butter cross "arms" to cover the mixture.
5. Fold both remaining "arms" over the top to form a parcel.
6. Enjoy immediately or refrigerate until ready to serve.

Variation:

Add 1/4 cup finely shredded red or green cabbage to the filling and increase the mayonnaise.

KALE SALAD WITH ROASTED YAMS

A delicious contrast of flavors and textures.

GLUTEN-FREE, NO SUGAR

Serves 6-8

2 pounds yams (orange)

3-4 large leaves fresh kale

1/4 cup peanut butter

1/2 teaspoons honey

2 tablespoons water

2-3 tablespoons lemon juice

2 garlic cloves, minced

1/8 teaspoon cayenne

1/4 teaspoon salt (if using unsalted peanut butter)

2 tablespoons coconut oil, melted

2 tablespoons goat cheese (or feta or gorgonzola)

2 tablespoons dried cranberries (optional)

1. Cut yams into bite-size pieces, coat with coconut oil, and place on cookie sheet. Bake at 425 degrees for 25 minutes or until tender.

2. In small bowl, whisk together peanut butter, honey, water, lemon juice, garlic, cayenne, and salt. Set aside.
3. Remove ribs from kale and discard. Slice leaves into narrow ribbons.
4. While still hot, toss yams with kale and cranberries. Add dressing and continue to toss lightly. Top with crumbled cheese.

BEET SALAD

A satisfying salad, pleasing to both the eye and the palate.

GLUTEN-FREE, SUGAR-FREE

Serves 1-2

3 cups romaine

1/4 cup chopped cucumber

3 dates, chopped

1/2 cup grapefruit sections, cut into thirds

1 medium cooked beet, cut into 1-inch cubes

1/4 cup goat cheese (optional)

1. Tear lettuce into bite-size pieces.
2. Toss all ingredients together. Serve with dressing (below).

Dressing

Makes approximately 1 1/3 cups.

2/3 cup oil

1/3 cup orange juice

2 teaspoons apple cider vinegar

1 1/2 tablespoons honey

2 tablespoons creamy peanut butter

1/2 teaspoon minced fresh ginger

2 teaspoons Bragg Liquid Aminos or soy sauce

1/2 teaspoon minced garlic

1/8 teaspoon salt.

Whisk together all ingredients until well-blended. Serve over salad.

STUFFED SPAGHETTI SQUASH WITH QUINOA AND SPICY PEANUT BUTTER SAUCE

A hearty, well-balanced meal when served with a green salad.

GLUTEN-FREE

Makes 3-4 servings.

1 medium spaghetti squash

1 cup cooked quinoa

1 can (14 oz.) black beans, drained and rinsed

1 tablespoon coconut or olive oil

2 cloves garlic

1/2 cup red onion, chopped

1 small jalapeño pepper, finely chopped

1 small red pepper, chopped

1/2 cup fresh mushrooms, sliced

1/2 tablespoon cumin

1/2 tablespoon chili powder

2 tablespoons soy sauce

1/4 cup peanut butter

1 teaspoon coconut sugar

Juice of 1 lime

2 tablespoons water

1/8 teaspoon cayenne

1/2 cup chopped cilantro, divided

1 cup grated cheddar cheese

1. On baking sheet, bake whole squash for 45-50 minutes at 375 degrees.
2. Cool for 20 minutes, then cut in half with sharp knife. Remove seeds and discard. With a fork, scrape flesh from sides of squash, forming long strands.
3. Sauté garlic, onion, peppers, and mushrooms in oil until soft. Add cumin   and chili powder and sauté 1 minute.
4. Stir in beans and quinoa. Carefully combine with the squash and half of the cilantro.
5. Whisk together peanut butter, soy sauce, lime juice, honey, and cayenne, and stir into the cooked vegetables. Pile into squash shells.
6. Sprinkle cheese on top and broil until cheese melts.

DESSERTS

PEANUT BUTTER CHOCOLATE MOUSSE

Rich, thick, delicious, and velvety-smooth. If you prefer a milk chocolate taste, substitute coconut milk for the water.

GLUTEN-FREE, DAIRY-FREE, SUGAR-FREE

Makes 1-2 servings

1/2 cup avocado

1/3 cup smooth peanut butter

1/3 cup maple syrup

1 1/2 tablespoons cacao

1 1/2 teaspoons vanilla extract

1/3 - 1/2 cup water

Add a few grains of salt if peanut butter is unsalted.

Blend all ingredients in blender. Chill well, about 2 hours.

NO-BAKE PEANUT BUTTER CHOCOLATE CHEESECAKE

An unbelievably good, dairy-free, almost-raw version of a favorite dessert.

DAIRY-FREE, GLUTEN-FREE, NO REFINED SUGAR

Serves 8-10

CRUST

2 cups raw cashew or macadamia nuts

1 cup pitted dates

2 tablespoons cacao

1. Process nuts and dates in food processor just until mixture holds together. Do not over-process.
2. Press onto bottom of 8-inch pie or cheesecake pan. Place in freezer while making filling.

FILLING

1 1/2 cups raw cashews, soaked for 2-4 hours

1/2 cup coconut oil, melted

1/2 cup maple syrup

1 1/2 tablespoons honey

1/2 cup smooth unsweetened peanut butter

1/2 cup cacao,

1 cup water

4 tablespoons vanilla extract

2 tablespoons lemon juice

Pinch of salt (if using unsalted peanut butter)

1. Process all ingredients in food processor or blender until smooth.
2. Pour over crust and freeze. Flavor is best after 24 hours.
3. Spread with topping and serve.

TOPPING

4 tablespoons creamy peanut butter

2 tablespoons coconut oil

2 tablespoons maple syrup

Place all ingredients in small bowl and whisk together.

TWO-LAYER PEANUT BUTTER GELATO

This is yummy as it is, but for an extra treat, pour Peanut Butter Chocolate Coconut Syrup over it (recipe below) and add sliced bananas.

GLUTEN-FREE, DAIRY-FREE, SUGAR-FREE

Makes 3-4 servings.

1 cup coconut milk

1 large (7-8 inch) ripe banana

1/2 cup salted peanut butter

1 teaspoon vanilla

2 tablespoons cacao

2 teaspoons agave syrup

1/2 teaspoon cinnamon (optional)

1. Blend milk, banana, peanut butter, and vanilla in blender until smooth. Remove about 2/3 cup of the mixture and place this in a shallow 2-cup container. Freeze.
2. Blend the cacao, agave syrup, and cinnamon into the remaining mixture. Refrigerate until first mixture is frozen, about 2 hours.

3. Pour cacao mixture over frozen first layer. Freeze 2-4 hours.

4. Remove from freezer at least 15 minutes before serving. This is best when eaten within two days.

PEANUT BUTTER CHOCOLATE COCONUT SYRUP

I like this syrup over bananas and chunks of peanut butter cookies. It's also great over gelato and ice cream.

GLUTEN-FREE, DAIRY-FREE, SUGAR-FREE

Makes about 3/4 cup.

2 tablespoons coconut oil

2 tablespoons peanut butter

2 rounded tablespoons cacao powder

5 teaspoons maple syrup

5-6 tablespoons water

1 teaspoon vanilla

With all ingredients at room temperature, blend or whisk together until smooth.

BUTTER TARTS

These are sweet and rich, and seem to improve with age. They will keep well up to 4 or 5 days.

GLUTEN-FREE, DAIRY-FREE, SUGAR-FREE

Makes 10-12 servings.

BASE

1 cup finely ground cashews

3/4 cup dates, coarsely chopped

1/8 cup (scant) coconut flour

1/2 tablespoon melted coconut oil

1/2 teaspoon vanilla

1-2 tablespoons coconut, cashew, or almond milk, if needed

1. Process nuts, flour, oil, and vanilla in food processor until blended.
2. While continuing to blend, slowly add dates.
3. Add milk if needed to hold mixture together when pressed between your fingers.
4. Press base down onto the bottom and slightly up the sides of a 9-inch pie plate.

FILLING

2 tablespoons peanut butter

2 tablespoons soft butter

1/4 cup coconut sugar

1/2 cup maple syrup

1 egg, lightly beaten

1/2 teaspoon vanilla

1/2 cup raisins

Pinch of salt

1. Process all ingredients except raisins in blender or food processor until   well-blended.
2. Add raisins and continue to process until mixed.
3. Spoon mixture over base, being sure that raisins are evenly distributed.
4. Bake at 400 degrees for 10 minutes. Reduce heat to 325 degrees and bake an additional 20-25 minutes or until filling is set.
5. When cool, cut into wedges and serve.

CHOCOLATE PEANUT BUTTER BANANA PIE

It's always an extra treat to have something nutritious taste so good. This luscious three-layer pie can be served chilled or frozen.

GLUTEN-FREE, DAIRY-FREE, SUGAR-FREE

Serves 8-10.

BASE

1 cup pecans

1 cup walnuts

1/2 cup pitted dates

4 tablespoons cacao powder

2 teaspoons vanilla extract

Pinch salt

1/2 cup smooth peanut butter, softened

1. Process nuts, dates, cacao, vanilla, and salt in food processor until mixture holds together.
2. Press onto the bottom and sides of 9-inch pie pan. Place in freezer for about 20 minutes.

3. Remove from freezer and spread with softened peanut butter. Return to freezer until firm.

FILLING

1/2 cup peanut butter

4 medium bananas

1/2 teaspoon vanilla

1. In blender or food processor, blend peanut butter, bananas, and vanilla until smooth.
2. Pour filling over peanut butter layer and return to freezer. When well-chilled, carefully spread with topping.

TOPPING

1/2 cup dates, soaked

3/4 cup avocado

1/4 cup maple syrup

1/2 teaspoon vanilla extract

6 tablespoons cacao powder

1/4 cup water or less (use as little as possible; this should be quite thick)

1. In blender or food processor, blend dates, avocado, syrup, vanilla, cacao, and water until smooth.
2. Spread over banana/peanut butter layer.
3. For best flavor, freeze for 24 hours. Remove from freezer 10-15 minutes before serving.

COCONUT CHOCOLATE PEANUT BUTTER ICE CREAM

Smooth, creamy, and delicious.

Makes 2-4 servings.

1 1/2 cup fresh raw coconut pieces

2 tablespoons cacao

1/4 cup peanut butter

1/4 cup pure maple syrup

1 tablespoon agave syrup

1 cup water

1/2 teaspoon vanilla

Blend all ingredients in blender until smooth. Freeze.

COOKIES, BARS, BROWNIES, AND FUDGE

PEANUT BUTTER SANDWICH COOKIES

Your choice of date or chocolate fillings. To make these gluten-free, I use buckwheat flour.

GLUTEN-FREE, SUGAR-FREE

Makes 3 dozen cookies.

2/3 cup butter

1 cup peanut butter

1 1/2 cup coconut sugar

2 eggs

1/2 cup flour

1 1/3 cups gluten-free oatmeal

2 teaspoons baking soda

1 teaspoon vanilla

3/4 teaspoon salt (if butter and peanut butter are unsalted)

Flour for flattening cookies

1. Combine butter, peanut butter, sugar, and eggs in food processor.

2. Form into balls and place on a greased or parchment-lined cookie sheet. Flatten with the bottom of a floured glass.
3. Bake at 360 degrees for 9-10 minutes. Do not over-bake.
4. When cool, make a sandwich with one of the fillings below. Double the filling recipe if you like extra in your sandwich.

Date Filling

Not too sweet.

1 cup chopped dates

1 tablespoon coconut sugar

2 teaspoons lemon juice

1/3 cup water

In small saucepan on low heat, simmer the dates, water, and sugar until the dates are soft and the water has been absorbed. Cool.

Chocolate Filling

An intense chocolate flavor.

1/4 cup coconut oil

1/4 cup cacao

1 tablespoon maple syrup

1/4 teaspoon vanilla

Pinch salt

Blend all ingredients until smooth.

NO-BAKE PEANUT BUTTER COOKIES

A quick, satisfying, raw version of an old favorite.

GLUTEN-FREE, DAIRY-FREE, SUGAR-FREE

1 cup raw almonds or almond meal

1 cup pitted dates

1/2 cup natural peanut butter

1 1/2 teaspoons vanilla extract

1/4 teaspoon salt (if peanut butter is unsalted)

Water

1. Process all ingredients in food processor or mix by hand until a dough is formed. Add a little water if needed.
2. Form into balls (approximately 1 1/4 inch diameter). Place on parchment-lined or greased cookie sheet. Gently press cookies with a fork to flatten.
3. Store in closed container in refrigerator.

PEANUT BUTTER CARROT RAISIN COOKIES

Cardamom beautifully complements the subtle flavors of the carrot and peanut butter and adds a spark of its own.

GLUTEN-FREE, SUGAR-FREE

Makes approximately 30 cookies.

1 cup ground carrots

1/2 cup butter

1/2 cup peanut butter

1 egg

1 cup coconut sugar

2 tablespoons water

2 cups buckwheat flour

2 teaspoons baking powder

1/2 teaspoon cinnamon

1/2 teaspoon ginger powder

1/4 teaspoon nutmeg

1/2 teaspoon cardamom

1/8 teaspoon salt (more if peanut butter is unsalted)

1 cup raisins

1 cup chopped walnuts (optional)

1. Grind carrots in food processor or grate by hand. Set aside.
2. Process butter, peanut butter, and egg until fluffy. Add sugar and continue to process. Add carrots and water and combine well.
3. In small bowl, combine flour, sugar, baking powder, spices, and salt. Add to butter mixture and mix well. Add raisins and walnuts and process until a soft dough is formed. Chill 15-20 minutes.
4. Drop by spoonfuls onto parchment-lined baking sheet.
5. Bake at 350 degrees for 10-12 minutes.

SPICY PEANUT BUTTER BROWNIES

If you like spices, you won't be able to resist these.

NO-BAKE, GLUTEN-FREE, DAIRY-FREE

Makes 16 pieces (2 inches square).

1 cup almonds

3 tablespoons coconut sugar

1/8 teaspoon salt

1/4 cup cacao powder

3/4 cup packed, pitted dates

2/3 cup creamy peanut butter

1/4 teaspoon cinnamon

1/4 teaspoon nutmeg

1/4 teaspoon cloves

1/4 teaspoon allspice

2 teaspoons vanilla

2 teaspoons water

1. In food processor, process almonds, sugar, cacao, and salt until they reach a flour-like consistency.
2. Add dates and process until they are broken down.

3. Add peanut butter, spices, vanilla, and water and process until the ingredients are evenly combined and dough holds together in your hand.

4. Press into 8 x 8 inch pan.

ONE-BITE BROWNIES WITH WALNUTS

Pop one of these into your mouth when you're in a hurry or want just a bite of something chocolatey and sweet for dessert. The rich flavor of cacao is intensified by the sharpness of cayenne.

NO-BAKE, DAIRY-FREE, SUGAR-FREE

Makes 12.

3/4 cup walnuts

7 Medjool dates, pitted

1/4 cup cacao powder

1 tablespoon peanut butter

1 teaspoon vanilla extract

1/8 teaspoon cayenne

Pinch of salt

Finely shredded coconut or ground nuts

1. Grind walnuts until fine. A food processor works well for this.
2. Add dates, cacao, vanilla, peanut butter, cayenne, and salt and process until smooth.

3. Place in freezer for a few minutes until mixture loses some of its stickiness and can easily be formed into bite-sized balls.

4. Roll balls in coconut or finely ground nuts. Store in freezer.

ONE-BITE BROWNIES WITH SUNFLOWER SEEDS

In these brownies, maca pairs well with the chocolate and sunflower seeds for an unusual flavor.

GLUTEN-FREE, DAIRY-FREE, SUGAR-FREE

Makes 12.

4 1/2 tablespoons ground sunflower seeds

1 1/2 tablespoons cacao

3 tablespoons peanut butter

1 1/2 teaspoons maca powder

3 dates

2 tablespoons agave

3/4 teaspoon vanilla extract

Pinch of salt

Ground sunflower seeds for coating

1. Grind sunflower seeds. A coffee grinder works well.
2. Process all ingredients in a food processor or mix by hand until mixture holds together.
3. Place in freezer for a few minutes until mixture loses some of its stickiness and can be easily

formed into 1-inch balls. Roll in ground sunflower seeds and store in freezer.

PEANUT BUTTER FUDGE

This yummy no-cook fudge can be made mostly with raw ingredients.

DAIRY-FREE, GLUTEN-FREE, SUGAR-FREE

Makes 16 one-inch square pieces.

1/2 cup crunchy peanut butter

12 Medjool or other large dates

1/2 cup ground pecans

3 tablespoons tahini

Pulse all ingredients in food processor or mix by hand until smooth except for peanut pieces. Refrigerate for a few hours before serving.

BUTTERSCOTCH PEANUT BUTTER FUDGE (LUMPY)

This doesn't fall into the "healthy" category. I include it for sentimental reasons—my kids loved it when they were growing up. I don't know the recipe source, but it was called "Lumpy." It's very rich, so you may want to cut the pieces very small—or you may not!

GLUTEN-FREE

Makes 16-24 pieces.

1/2 cup butter
1 cup smooth peanut butter
2 11-ounce packages butterscotch morsels (chips)
3 cups miniature marshmallows

1. Melt butter, peanut butter, and butterscotch morsels over hot water, stirring constantly until smooth. You can use a double boiler or a bowl set on a rack in a pan of hot water. Do not let the water boil.
2. When smooth, remove from heat source and cool.
3. Fold marshmallows into cooled mixture until well-mixed.
4. Place in 8 x 8 inch pan and chill in refrigerator.

AFTERWARD

I hope you enjoy these recipes. May they continue to satisfy your peanut butter cravings for years to come! I loved creating them and still salivate when I read them. I wish I'd kept track of the number of jars of peanut butter I used while working on this book—I might be astounded if I knew the amount of peanut butter I actually consumed.

I would love to hear your comments. Sincere feedback is always welcome. If you'd like to leave a review, go to my book at: *www.amazon.com/books* and click on "Write a customer review."

Another book by Joyce Mackie: "Walking The Thames River Path, A Solo Journey Of Adventure And Self-Discovery" available at: *www.amazon.com/books* .

BIBLIOGRAPHY

Bernard, Jan. *Peanut Butter Before The Store*. The Child's World US, 2012.

Erlbach, Arlene. *Peanut Butter, How It's Made*. Lerner Publications, 1994.

Kaufman, William I. *The Peanut Butter Cookbook*. New York Simon and Schuster, 1977.

Krampner, Jon. *Creamy and Crunchy, An Informal History of Peanut Butter, The All-American food*. Columbia University Press, 2013.

Zisman, Larry and Honey. *The Great American Peanut Butter Book, Over 150 Delicious Ways to Enjoy America's Favorite Food*. New York St. Martin's Press, 1985.

Websites:

National Peanut Board *(www.nationalpeanutboard.org)*
The Peanut Institute *(www.peanut-institute.org)*

ACKNOWLEDGEMENTS

I would like to thank my family for their support and encouragement, and for always taking the time to answer my requests for feedback. A special thank you to my sister Dee for recipe testing, and for her valuable input.

I am grateful to my co-workers for their willingness to try my latest concoctions. In particular, I would like to thank Sarah Corry, a fellow peanut butter lover, who always cheered me on, and liked everything I made, even when it needed improvement.

My appreciation to my editor, Marian Kelly, for her insightful comments and helpful suggestions, and to Steve Barrow for his patience and perseverance in translating my hazy vision into the cover design.

Printed in Great Britain
by Amazon